SHORT STORIES IN ENGLISH/ITALIAN

UNLOCK IGNITE & TRANSFORM YOUR LANGUAGE
SKILLS WITH CONTEMPORARY ROMANCE
BOOK 13

LAURA MARIANI

PEOPLE
ALCHEMIST

ABOUT THE AUTHOR

Laura Mariani, also known as Laura (LA) Mariani, is a genre-straddling author of non-fiction success books for women and contemporary romance.

She is a Change and Transformation expert, Fellow of the Chartered Institute of Personnel & Development (**FCIPD**), Fellow of the Australian Human Resources Institute (**FAHRI**), Fellow of the Institute of Leadership & Management (**FInstLM**), Member of the Society of Human Resources Management (**SHRM**) and Member of the Change Institute.

Her **non-fiction books** combine positive psychology motivation with a healthy dose of practical tips - Change & Transformation made easy to Unlock Ignite & Transform your life, business, or career.

As Laura (LA.) Mariani she writes **Short, Steamy Romance** with strong alpha males, fierce heroines, and sweet endings.

When not busy writing, you can find Laura exploring London's vibrant streets or traveling far away places, always seeking new horizons and cultural experiences.

SULL' AUTRICE

Laura Mariani, nota anche come Laura (L.A.) Mariani, è un'autrice che spazia tra i generi di saggistica di successo per donne e romanzi rosa contemporanei.

Laura è Fellow del Chartered Institute of Personnel & Development (FCIPD), Fellow dell'Australian Human Resources Institute (FAHRI), Fellow dell'Institute of Leadership & Management (FInstLM), Membro della Society of Human Resources Management (SHRM) e membro del Change Institute.

I suoi libri di saggistica combinano la motivazione della psicologia positiva con una sana dose di consigli pratici: cambiamento e trasformazione resi facili per Unlock Ignite & Transform la tua vita, il tuo business o la tua carriera.

Con lo pseudonimo Laura (LA.) Mariani scrive romanzi rosa brevi e bollenti con forti maschi alfa, eroine feroci e finali dolci.

Quando non è impegnata a scrivere, puoi trovare Laura che esplora le vivaci strade di Londra o viaggia in luoghi lontani, sempre alla ricerca di nuovi orizzonti ed esperienze culturali.

Contact information

For everything Change & Transformation: www.thepeoplelchemist.com

For everything romance: https://www.amazon.com/author/l.a. mariani

You can also follow her on:

- LinkedIn: https://www.linkedin.com/in/lauramariani-fcipd/
- Twitter: https://twitter.com/PeopleAlchemist
- Instagram: https://www.instagram.com/lauramariani_author/

Informazioni di contatto

Per tutto ciò che riguarda il cambiamento e la trasformazione: www.thepeoplelchemist.com

Per stories romantiche contemporanee: https://www.amazon.com/author/l.a.mariani

Puoi anche seguirla su:

- LinkedIn: https://www.linkedin.com/in/lauramariani-fcipd/
- Twitter: https://twitter.com/PeopleAlchemist
- Instagram: https://www.instagram.com/lauramariani_author/

ThePeopleAlchemist Press publishes self help, inspirational and transformational books, resources and products to help #TheWomanAlchemist in every woman to change her life/ career and transmute any circumstance into gold, a bit like magic to **Unlock Ignite Transform.**

ISBN: 978-1-917104-20-3

ThePeopleAlchemist Press pubblica libri, risorse e prodotti di self-help, d'
ispirazione e trasformazione per aiutare # **TheWomanAlchemist** in ogni donna a
cambiare la sua vita / carriera e trasmutare qualsiasi circostanza in oro, un po' come
per magia per **Unlock Ignite Transform**.

ISBN: 978-1-917104-20-3

INTRODUCTION

Welcome to the series **Unlock Ignite & Transform** your language skills reading short stories.

When we are born, every possibility exists to pronounce and learn every sound in every language. But early on, our brains lay down neural pathways that interweave with the sounds we hear daily, eliminating sounds and words from other languages.

The **Unlock Ignite Transform** series aims to unlock the power of your subconscious mind and assist in resurfacing those abilities that have always been at your disposal.

Our subconscious is ready to execute any message we send and reproduce it in our physical reality, like a printer.

In this book, you will not find any dictionary, synonyms or grammar points because that would signal to your subconscious mind that you are *learning* and *practising* a new language.

Instead, we want to send the message that you are *reading* in two languages because you *already know them* both and you

INTRODUZIONE

Benvenuto alla series **Unlock Ignite & Transform**a le tue abilità linguistiche leggendo racconti.

Quando nasciamo, esiste in noi ogni possibilità di pronunciare e imparare ogni suono in ogni lingua. Ma presto i nostri cervelli stabiliscono percorsi neurali che si intrecciano con i suoni e parole che ascoltiamo quotidianamente, eliminando suoni e parole di altre lingue.

La serie **Unlock Ignite Transform** ha lo scopo di sbloccare il potere del vostro subconscio e aiutarvi a far riemergere quelle abilità che sono sempre state a vostra disposizione.

Il nostro subconscio è pronto a eseguire qualsiasi messaggio che inviamo e riprodurlo nella nostra realtà fisica, come una stampante.

In questo libro non troverete alcun dizionario, sinonimo o punto grammaticale perché ciò segnalerebbe al vostro subconscio che state *imparando* e *praticando* una nuova lingua.

Invece, vogliamo inviare il messaggio che state leggendo in

are *bilingual*.

The series offers parallel text in both English and Italian to enjoy contemporary literature in both languages (there is no need to constantly refer back to a dictionary because you *already ARE bilingual*).

The more you get the message to your subconscious mind that is *normal* for you to read either language, the more your subconscious will try to demonstrate to you that this is indeed correct.

The thirteenth short story in the series is **It Was Always You.**

His hands were wet and sticky; he was so nervous. She was there. She was actually there. He started walking towards her when she sprinted into his arms.

"I guess you are happy to see me," she smiled.

"Cheeky," he smiled too. "Obviously."

"You came," holding her face in his hands. "You are here. That is all that matter."

Happy reading!

due lingue perché *le conoscete già entrambe e siete bilingue.*

La serie offre testi paralleli sia in inglese che in italiano per godersi la letteratura contemporanea in entrambe le lingue (non c'è bisogno di fare costantemente riferimento a un dizionario perché *SEI già bilingue*).

Più il vostro subconscio riceve il messaggio che è normale per voi leggere in entrambe le lingue, più cercherà di dimostrarvi che questo è davvero corretto.

Il tredicesimo racconto incluso in questa serie è **Eri Sempre Tu.**

Le sue mani erano bagnate e appiccicose; era così nervoso. Lei era lì. Lei era davvero lì. Aveva iniziato a muoversi verso di lei quando lei scattò tra le su
e braccia.

"Suppongo che tu sia felice di vedermi," sorrise.

"Sfacciata," sorrise anche lui. "Ovviamente."

"Sei venuta," tenendole il viso tra le mani. "Sei qui. Questo è tutto ciò che conta."

Buona lettura!

IT WAS ALWAYS YOU

"Ms Arkin? Ms ..." Gabrielle she heard as she was walking back toward the hotel. She turned around and saw George rushing toward her, out of breath, waving.

"Ms Arkin?" he said again.

She had never been happier to see someone.
  "George, so happy to see you," smiling through her tears.

He could see how distraught she was and updated her on the events as quickly as possible.

"I am here to take you to the hospital; if you want to go, that is?" he asked.

"Yes, yes," Gabrielle nodded.

"My car is there," he pointed.

George was looking at Gabrielle through the rearview mirror. She looked worried and tearing up, but at least she was here. He had his doubts but never shared them with Mr Wonderful.

"Is it far?" she asked.

"No, only 3 kilometres. There is just some evening traffic to go through."

She nodded.

ERI SEMPRE TU

"Signora Arkin? Signora..." sentì Gabrielle mentre tornava verso l'albergo. Si voltò e vide George correre verso di lei, senza fiato, salutandola.

"Signorina Arkin?" disse di nuovo.

Non era mai stata così felice di vedere qualcuno come adesso. "George, sono così felice di vederti," sorridendo tra le lacrime.

Poteva vedere quanto fosse sconvolta e la aggiornò sugli eventi il più rapidamente possibile.

"Sono qui per portarla all'ospedale; se vuole andare ovviamente?" chiese.

"Sì, sì," annuì Gabrielle.

"La mia macchina è lì," indicò.

George guardava Gabrielle attraverso lo specchietto retrovisore. Sembrava preoccupata e in lacrime, ma almeno era qui. Aveva i suoi dubbi ma non li ha mai condivisi con Mr Wonderful.

"È lontano?" lei chiese.

"No, solo 3 chilometri. C'è solo un po' di traffico serale da percorrere."

Lei annuì.

As they entered the building, Gabrielle looked lost. Thank God George was there and knew where to go.

"This way," he said. Then, as they were walking, George saw Mr Wonderful in the seating area, his head in his hands, surrounded by his brothers. The wait had been agonising.

Waiting for Gabrielle.
Waiting for the doctors to tell them something. Anything.

"Sir?"

He looked up and saw George, alone. His eyes searched. And then, just behind him, Gabrielle.

His hands were wet and sticky; he was so nervous. She was there. She was actually there. He started walking towards her when she sprinted into his arms. The long passionate embrace, their cheeks touching, his breath on her neck, her breath in his ear. He was so aroused that he dared not release her from his embrace. He was so hard that he'd feared it'd show.

I guess you are happy to see me", she smiled.

"Cheeky," he smiled too. "Obviously."

His sparkling blue eyes were full of unreleased tears.

"You came; you are here. Sorry, I had to leave," he said.

"I was late; I am sorry I was late," Gabrielle apologised.

"it was not your fault, baby," holding her face in his hands. "You are here. That is all that matter," he added.

Quando entrarono nell'edificio, Gabrielle sembrava persa. Grazie a Dio, George era lì e sapeva dove andare.

"Da questa parte," le disse. Poi, mentre camminavano, George vide Mr Wonderful nell'area salotto, con la testa tra le mani, circondato dai suoi fratelli. L'attesa era stata straziante.

Aspettando Gabriele.

Aspetto che i dottori dicano loro qualcosa. Nulla.

"Signore?"

Alzò lo sguardo e vide George, solo. I suoi occhi cercarono. E poi, proprio dietro di lui, Gabrielle.

Le sue mani erano bagnate e appiccicose; era così nervoso. Lei era lì. Lei era davvero lì. Aveva iniziato a muoversi verso di lei quando lei scattò tra le sue braccia. Il lungo abbraccio appassionato, le loro guance che si toccavano, il respiro di lui sul collo di lei, il respiro di lei nel suo orecchio. Era così eccitato che non osava lasciarla andare dal suo abbraccio. Inoltre era così eccitato che temeva che si potesse vedere.

"Suppongo che tu sia felice di vedermi," sorrise.
    "Sfacciata," sorrise anche lui. "Ovviamente."
    I suoi scintillanti occhi azzurri erano pieni di lacrime non espresse.

"Sei venuta; sei qui. Scusa, ho dovuto andarmene," disse.

"Ero in ritardo, mi dispiace di essere in ritardo," si scusò Gabrielle.

"Non è stata colpa tua, piccola," tenendole il viso tra le mani. "Sei qui. Questo è tutto ciò che conta," aggiunse.

"I'm so sorry about your brother," she asked.

"Yes, thank you."

"Do you know ..?"

"Not yet; we are waiting."

Mr Wonderful waved at George.

"Thank you," moving his lips.

His brothers were starting to gather around them when the surgeon came out of the swinging doors. The doctor went straight toward Mr Wonderful.

"He is still in critical condition, Viscount. He has suffered a brain injury. We had to medically induce a coma to prevent intracranial hypertension and allow the brain to recuperate."

They all stood there, stunned.

"There is nothing you can do here. He is in intensive care. We will call you if anything happens," the doctor added.

"We are not leaving," voices rising.

"Thank you, Doctor," Mr Wonderful took charge.

"There is no reason for all of us to stay. We can take turns," he said.

"We can stay," Gabrielle intervened, holding Mr Wonderful's arm. She knew he wanted to stay but wouldn't say because of her. He turned to look at her. "We can do the first shift," she continued.

"Yes," taking it from where she left off, "You all have families waiting for you, go."

"Mi dispiace tanto per tuo fratello," chiese.

"Si Grazie."

"Sai ..?"

"Non ancora, stiamo aspettando."

Mr Wonderful fece un cenno a George.

"Grazie," muovendo le labbra.

I suoi fratelli stavano cominciando a raccogliersi intorno a loro quando il chirurgo uscì dalle porte a battente. Il dottore andò dritto verso Mr Wonderful.

"È ancora in condizioni critiche, Visconte. Ha subito una lesione cerebrale. Abbiamo dovuto indurre un coma medico per prevenire l'ipertensione endocranica e permettere al cervello di riprendersi."

Rimasero tutti lì, sbalorditi.

"Non c'è niente che potete fare qui. È in terapia intensiva. Vi chiameremo se succede qualcosa," aggiunse il medico.

"Non ce ne andiamo," voci che si alzavano.

"Grazie, dottore," prese in carico Mr Wonderful. "Non c'è motivo per tutti noi di restare. Possiamo fare i turni," disse.

"Possiamo restare noi," intervenì Gabrielle, tenendo forte il braccio di Mr Wonderful. Lei sapeva che lui voleva restare, ma non l'avrebbe detto a causa sua. Si voltò a guardarla. "Possiamo fare il primo turno," continuò.

"Sì," riprendendo da dove si era interrotta, "Avete tutti delle famiglie che vi aspettano, andate."

"I'll call if anything happens," he continued.

"I'll do the night. I'll come back later after the children are in bed," his brother Paul said.

After some more talks and hugs, the others left.

"Sir, shall I wait for you?" George was still there.

"There's no need, George, thank you. We will take a cab," Mr Wonderful responded.

"They were finally alone. Alone in a hospital waiting room. Not exactly what he had planned," he was thinking, feeling guilty.

"You hungry?" he asked her.

"Not really, but I could do with a coffee," Gabrielle replied.

"It's machine coffee," knowing how particular she was about coffee.

"It's fine." She had yet to let go of his arm.

They walked together to the dispensing machine and settled down in the corner of the waiting area.

Mr Wonderful was thinking how much he wanted her right there and then and feeling totally inappropriate for it.

She was sitting beside him, looking at him, holding the plastic coffee cup with both her hands. A quizzing look in her eyes.

"Chiamerò se succede qualcosa," lui poi continuò.

"Farò io la notte. Tornerò più tardi, dopo che i bambini sono a letto," disse suo fratello Paul.

Dopo altri parole scambiate e abbracci, gli altri se ne andarono.

"Signore, devo aspettarvi?" Giorgio era ancora lì.

"Non ce n'è bisogno, George, grazie. Prendiamo un taxi," rispose Mr Wonderful.

"Finalmente erano soli. Soli nella sala d'attesa di un ospedale. Non esattamente quello che aveva programmato," stava pensando, sentendosi in colpa.

"Ha fame?" le chiese.

"Non proprio, ma mi farebbe piacere un caffè," rispose Gabrielle.

"È il caffè della macchina," sapendo quanto fosse particolare con il caffè.

"Va bene." Doveva ancora lasciare andare il suo braccio.

Andarono insieme al distributore automatico e si sistemarono nell'angolo della sala d'attesa.

Mr Wonderful stava pensando a quanto la desiderava proprio lì e in quel momento e si sentiva totalmente in colpa per questo.

Era seduta accanto a lui, lo guardava, tenendo la tazzina di plastica del caffè con entrambe le mani. Uno sguardo interrogativo nei suoi occhi.

"When I arrived at the Empire State, I asked for you, and the man didn't seem to know you," she blurted out, unable to hold her curiosity any longer.

He had a puzzled look, and his eyebrows crumpled.

"I asked for Mr Vitale. He called you Fitzwilliam. You are not some double agent spy, are you?" she added, trying to make a joke of it. "Had he been hiding something from her?" she was, however, thinking.

"You are watching and reading far too much detective drama," he smiled.

"You are both right," he added. Gabrielle looked even more perplexed. His hand was on her thigh, caressing her; she couldn't think straight.

"Long story," Mr Wonderful went on.

Gabrielle was getting warmer by the minute, the gentle stroke arousing her like crazy.

"We have time," she smiled, "I always assumed you were kind of Italian origins. Fitzwilliam is not very Italian."

"Italian?" a quizzical look on his face, " Ah!' recognising what she meant, "No. It was Vitalik. My maternal grandparents changed it when they arrived in the United States from Russia. They settled around Brooklyn, so Vitale seemed appropriate."

"She smelled so good," he was thinking, imagining what she was wearing underneath her cashmere jumper.

"Quando sono arrivata all'Empire State, ho chiesto di te, e l'uomo sembrava non conoscerti," sbottò lei, incapace di trattenere oltre la sua curiosità.

Lui aveva uno sguardo perplesso e le sopracciglia aggrottate.

"Ho chiesto del signor Vitale. Invece lui ti ha chiamato Fitzwilliam. Non sei una spia a doppio gioco, vero?" aggiunse, cercando di farne uno scherzo. "Le aveva nascosto qualcosa?" stava però pensando.

"Stai guardando e leggendo troppi drammi polizieschi," sorrise.

"Avete ragione entrambi," aggiunse poi. Gabrielle sembrava ancora più perplessa. La sua mano era sulla sua coscia, accarezzandola; non riusciva a pensare lucidamente.

"Lunga storia," continuò Mr Wonderful.

Gabrielle si stava riscaldando di minuto in minuto, la carezza gentile la stava eccitava come una matta.

"Abbiamo tempo," sorrise, "ho sempre pensato che fossi di origini italiane. Fitzwilliam non è un cognome molto italiano."

"Italiano?" uno sguardo interrogativo sul suo volto, "Ah!" riconoscendo ciò che voleva dire, "No. Era Vitalik. I miei nonni materni lo cambiarono quando arrivarono negli Stati Uniti dalla Russia. Si stabilirono intorno a Brooklyn, quindi Vitale sembrava appropriato."

"Ha un profumo così buono," stava pensando, immaginando cosa indossasse sotto il suo maglione di cachemire.

"My parents were never married," he continued, trying to keep together.

"My father was some aristocrat from Ireland who wanted to be bohemian and independent from his family obligations. So, he moved to the U.S. to escape his family and do 'his thing'. He met my mother, and things progressed from there," he looked bitter.

"One kid after another, they soon found themselves with five children. I am the eldest."

Gabrielle's eyes were open wide. He had told her before about the father leaving.

"One set of twins," he continued.

"Well, between his gambling and womanising and all the responsibilities, life was too hard for him," Mr Wonderful said sarcastically.

"One day, he just left, took all his things, and we never saw him again. He returned to his father with his tail between his legs, begged for forgiveness (and money), and married some other aristocrat."

Gabrielle put the cup of coffee on the small table in the waiting area and wrapped herself around his arm.

"He must have worked out more than usual. His muscles were even stronger and more compact," she thought. "STOP IT, Gabri".

"They couldn't have children. Then his wife died, and he started getting sick eight years ago. He came clean and told his father he had children after all—he had an heir to the family name," he went on.

"I miei genitori non si erano mai sposati," continuò, cercando di restare calmo.

"Mio padre era un aristocratico irlandese che voleva essere un bohémien e indipendente dai suoi obblighi familiari. Quindi si era trasferito negli Stati Uniti per sfuggire alla sua famiglia e fare 'le sue cose'. Qui incontrò mia madre e le cose sono andate avanti da lì," sembrava amareggiato.

"Un bambino dopo l'altro, presto si ritrovarono con cinque figli. Io sono il maggiore."

Gli occhi di Gabrielle erano spalancati. Le aveva già detto della partenza del padre.

"Una coppia di gemelli", aveva aggiunto.

"Beh, tra il suo gioco d'azzardo, essere un donnaiolo e tutte le responsabilità, la vita era troppo dura per lui," disse Mr Wonderful in maniera sarcastica.

"Un giorno se ne andò, dopo over preso tutte le sue cose e non ci siamo più rivisti. Ritornò da suo padre con la coda tra le gambe, chiese perdono (e denaro) e si sposò con un' aristocratica."

Gabrielle posò la tazza di caffè sul tavolino nella sala d'attesa e si strinse al suo braccio.

"Deve essersi allenato più del solito. I suoi muscoli erano ancora più forti e compatti," pensò. "Smettila, Gabri".

"Non sono riusciti ad avere figli. Poi sua moglie morì e, otto anni fa, lui incominciò ad ammalarsi. Era stato sincero e detto a suo padre che dopotutto aveva dei figli: aveva un erede del cognome," continuò.

"Wow," Gabrielle blurted out.

"Yes, can you believe it? He never told them? My grandparents never knew about us until then. My father used an alias in the U.S."

"Sounds like a movie," Gabrielle said.

He continued to caress her longer, deeper strokes inside the thigh, up .... and down...

"My father passed away shortly after his revelation. I got to know my grandfather for a while before he also passed away three years ago. My paternal grandmother is still with us."

"Viscount?" she recalled the doctor calling him.

"When my grandfather died, the title passed on to me, the firstborn," Mr Wonderful continued, "I am still getting used to it."

"Go on, tell me," Gabrielle was curious.

"Viscount Thomas Darcy Vitale Fitzwilliam III," he said.

"Don't ..." his finger on the tip of her nose, " don't laugh .... "

"Darcy Fitzwilliam?" Gabrielle was amused.

"Not funny. My mother was a big Austen fan. I'm grateful to him for at least one thing: he stopped her from naming me, Darcy."

"Guess?" she then asked. Mr Wonderful looked puzzled.

"Guess my middle name," she went on.

"Wow," sbottò Gabrielle.

"Sì, da non credere! Non gliel'aveva mai detto? I miei nonni non sapevano di noi fino ad allora. Mio padre aveva usato uno pseudonimo negli Stati Uniti."

"Sembra un film," disse Gabrielle.

Continuò ad accarezzarla con tocchi più lunghi e profondi all'interno della coscia, su... e giù...

"Mio padre morì poco dopo la sua rivelazione. Ho avuto l'opportunità di conoscere mio nonno per un po' prima che anche lui venisse a mancare tre anni fa. Mia nonna paterna è ancora con noi."

"Visconte?" Si ricordava che il dottore lo aveva chiamato.

"Quando è morto mio nonno, il titolo è passato a me, il primogenito," proseguì Mr Wonderful, "mi sto ancora abituando."

"Dai, dimmi," Gabrielle era curiosa.

"Visconte Thomas Darcy Vitale Fitzwilliam III," disse.

"Non..." le mise un dito sulla punta del naso, "non ridere... ."

"Darcy Fitzwilliam?" Gabrielle si stava divertendo infine.

"Non è divertente. Mia madre era una grande fan dell' Austen. Gli sono grato per almeno una cosa: le ha impedito darmi il nome Darcy."

"Indovina?" Lei chiese. Mr Wonderful sembrava perplesso. "Indovina il mio secondo nome," continuò.

"Not Elizabeth, is it?" with a quizzical look.

"Indeed it is. Nothing to do with Austen. I am named after my two grandmothers: Gabrielle and Elizabeth."

"If we had known, we could have just skipped to the end of the story," she said, resting her head on his chest, his arm around her.

"Hello, love birds," Paul startled them; he was back.

"How is Mickey?" he inquired.

"Still no news," Mr Wonderful responded.

"It is time for the two of you to go," Paul proceeded. "Go, go; I'll call if there is any news," he added to reassure them.

"We will be close by."

"Ok."

"See you in the morning."

They walked out of the hospital gloating, their feet almost not touching the ground; they were hungry for each, literally starving.

Mr Wonderful grabbed a taxi as it was passing by.
    "The Langham, Fifth Avenue," he said.

Of course, such a short ride did not amuse the taxi driver, but the $ 50 tip seemed to appease him—a lot. They arrived at the hotel shortly after. Gabrielle remembered she still needed to check-in.

"You'll be fine," he said.

"Elizabeth no, vero?" con uno sguardo interrogativo.

"In effetti lo è. Niente a che fare con Austen. Prendo il nome dalle mie due nonne: Gabrielle ed Elizabeth."

"Se l'avessimo saputo, saremmo potuti saltare alla fine della storia," disse, appoggiando la testa sul suo petto, il suo braccio intorno a lei.

"Ciao, piccioncini," Paul li fece trasalire; era tornato.

"Come sta Mickey?" chiese.

"Ancora nessuna notizia," rispose Mr Wonderful.

"È ora che voi due andiate," proseguì Paul. "Andate, andate, chiamo se ci sono novità," aggiunse per rassicurarli.

"Saremo vicini."

"OK."

"Ci vediamo in mattinata."

Uscirono dall'ospedale with great pleasure, i loro piedi quasi non toccavano terra; erano affamati l'uno dell'altro, letteralmente affamati. Mr Wonderful prese un taxi mentre passava. "The Langham, Fifth Avenue," disse.

Certo, una corsa così breve non aveva fatto molto piacere al tassista, ma la mancia di $ 50 sembrava di averlo placato, molto. Arrivarono in albergo poco dopo. Gabrielle si ricordò che doveva ancora fare il check-in.

"No importa," lui le disse.

"Viscount, so pleased to see you," Mr Wonderful nodded, "Ms Arkin, your luggage is in your room," the concierge said as he handed her the key.

"Welcome, and have a pleasant stay."

They both rushed to the lift, dying to be alone.

She couldn't open and close the bedroom door behind them fast enough.

He started kissing her face and her neck, caressing her breast.

Gabrielle yanked his jacket off his shoulder and onto the floor.

His hands down to her waist, unzipping her jeans.

She undid his belt and the zip and pulled his trousers and boxers down his tights. Their trousers down their ankles, they started moving, hopping towards the bed, kissing, panting.

"Shit," they tumbled on the floor. It always seemed so easy in the movies, where everything happens so smoothly, not so much in real life.

Gabrielle was on top of Mr Wonderful. "Ouch," she moaned.

"You OK?" he asked as he kicked his trousers off him.

"Yes," she replied. He got up, stark naked from his waist down, pulled her onto his shoulder, and then threw her on the bed. Their lovemaking was unbridled, unrestricted, and wild. And quick. The long wait at the hospital a prolonged and agonising foreplay. They lay there exhausted, still half-dressed, the bed covers all over the floor, neither saying anything. For the first time, there was nothing to add. They were with each other exactly where they were meant to be.

"Visconte, siamo così felice di vedervi," Mr Wonderful annuì, "Signora Arkin, il suo bagaglio è nella sua stanza," disse il portiere mentre le consegnava la chiave.

"Benvenuta e buon soggiorno."

Entrambi si precipitarono all'ascensore, morendo dalla voglia di restare soli. Non riusciva ad aprire e chiudere la porta della camera da letto dietro di loro abbastanza in fretta. Lui cominciò a baciarle il viso e il collo, accarezzandole il seno.

Gabrielle gli strappò la giacca dalla spalla e la fece cadere sul pavimento.

Le mani di lui sulla sua vita, aprendole la cerniera dei jeans. Lei gli slacciò la cintura e la zip e gli abbassò i pantaloni e i boxer. Con i pantaloni giù alle caviglie, iniziarono a muoversi, saltellando verso il letto, baciandosi, ansimando.

"Merda," rotolando sul pavimento. Sembrava sempre così facile nei film, dove tutto accade senza intoppi, non così tanto nella vita reale.

Gabrielle era sopra Mr Wonderful. "Ahi," gemette.

"Tutto ok?" Le chiese mentre si toglieva a calci i pantaloni.

"Sì," rispose lei. Si alzò, completamente nudo dalla vita in giù, se la tirò sulla spalla e poi la gettò sul letto. Il loro fare l'amore era questa volta sfrenato, senza restrizioni e selvaggio. E veloce. La lunga attesa in ospedale era stato un preliminare prolungato e straziante. Rimasero lì esausti, ancora semivestiti, le coperte del letto dappertutto sul pavimento, nessuno dei due diceva niente. Per la prima volta non c'era niente da aggiungere. Erano l'uno con l'altro esattamente dove dovevano essere.

"I need to shower, " Gabrielle said after a while.

"Can I join you?" he asked with a cheeky smile.

"I was hoping you would," she added. They jumped into a hot, long shower, Mr Wonderful working his magic with the shower head.

"Oh Tom, God Tom," she shouted.

"Not God, just Tom. But if you insist, though, Viscount will do," he said, flashing a smile.

She was too involved even to laugh.

"I have been perfecting my shower skill, you like?" he added.

"Love them!" Gabrielle screamed.

Their lovemaking lasted off and on all night, not a wink of sleep, both sustained by adrenaline. The sun was rising in New York.

"Do you want to get some sleep while I go back to the hospital? I must be exhausted," Mr Wonderful asked thoughtfully.

"I'll come with you; plenty of time to sleep," Gabrielle answered, not wanting to be apart from him, not even for a minute, especially now that she could be there for him like he always had for her.

The next few days went by, long days and nights at the hospital and family get-togethers. Then, one day, Michael recovered and was moved out of intensive care into a private room. After that, life started to get back to normal.

"Ho bisogno di farmi una doccia," disse Gabrielle dopo un po'.

"Posso unirmi a te?" chiese con un sorriso sfacciato.

"Speravo che lo facessi," lei aggiunse. Si tuffarono in una lunga e calda doccia, Mr Wonderful faceva la sua magia con il soffione.

"Oh Tom, Dio, Tom," lei gridava.

"Non Dio, solo Tom. Ma se insisti, però, Viscount andrà bene," disse, sorridendo.

Era troppo coinvolta anche per ridere.

"Ho perfezionato il mio talento nella doccia, ti piace?" aggiunse.
"L'adoro!" urlò Gabriella.

Il loro amore durò tutta la notte, senza un battito di ciglia, entrambi sostenuti dall'adrenalina.

Il sole stava sorgendo a New York.

"Vuoi dormire un po' mentre torno in ospedale? Devo essere esausta," chiese pensieroso Mr Wonderful.

"Vengo con te; c'è un sacco di tempo per dormire," rispose Gabrielle, non volendo separarsi da lui, nemmeno per un minuto, soprattutto ora che poteva essere lì per lui come lui era sempre stato per lei.

I giorni successivi passarono, lunghi giorni e notti in ospedale e riunioni di famiglia. Poi, un giorno, Michael cominciò a riprendersi fu trasferito dalla terapia intensiva in una stanza privata. Dopo di che, la vita aveva iniziato a tornare alla normalità.

Gabrielle had fit in smoothly with the family and got to know Mr Wonderful's grandmother via FaceTime. But, unfortunately, she was too fragile to travel from Ireland.

"Where did you hide this lovely girl Thomas?" she asked.

"You both must come over as soon as Michael is better for 'you know what'," wink wink, she said one day with a twinkle in her eye.

"What was that?" Gabrielle asked once the call was over.

"What?" he replied, pretending nothing had happened.

"You know, she said 'for you know what'. You know what, what?"

Mr Wonderful looked deeply into her eyes and took a small Tiffany box out of his pocket. He had been carrying it around since she arrived. He had planned a grand proposal at the top of the Empire State Building; a quartet of violinists, champagne, and red roses, but then the call, Michael, everything. Since then, he had been waiting for the right time.

He opened the box and went down on one knee.

"Baby, will you marry me?"

The ring was an exquisite 18K Tiffany Schlumberger engagement ring with diamonds and emeralds, which he had searched and searched for since they met. Gabrielle recognised the vintage piece from the Faerber collection; she started crying uncontrollably.

"Yes, yes," nodding.

"It was always you. It was always you."

Gabrielle si era adattata perfettamente alla famiglia e aveva conosciuto la nonna di Mr Wonderful tramite FaceTime. Sfortunatamente, era troppo fragile per viaggiare dall'Irlanda.

"Dove avevi nascosto questa adorabile ragazza Thomas?" lei chiese.

"Dovete venire entrambi non appena Michael sta meglio per 'sai cosa'," occhiolino, disse un giorno con un luccichio negli occhi.

"Che cos'era quell'espressione?" chiese Gabrielle una volta terminata la telefonata.

"Che cosa?" rispose, facendo finta di niente.

"Sai, ha detto 'perché sai cosa'. Sai cosa, cosa?"

Mr Wonderful la guardò profondamente negli occhi e tirò fuori dalla tasca una scatolina di Tiffany. Lo portava in giro da quando era arrivata. Aveva pianificato una grande proposta in cima all'Empire State Building; un quartetto di violinisti, champagne e rose rosse, ma poi la chiamata, Michael, tutto. Da allora, aveva aspettato il momento giusto. Aprì la scatola e si inginocchiò.

"Tesoro, mi vuoi sposare?"

L'anello era uno squisito anello di fidanzamento , un Tiffany Schlumberger da 18 carati con diamanti e smeraldi, che aveva cercato e cercato da quando si erano conosciuti. Gabrielle riconobbe il pezzo vintage della collezione Faerber; iniziò a piangere in modo incontrollabile.

"Sì, sì," annuendo.

"Eri sempre tu. Eri sempre tu la mia sola e unica."

QUOTE

" Love isn't perfect;
It isn't a fairytale or a storybook and
it doesn't always come easy.
Love is overcoming obstacles, facing challenges,
fighting to be together , holding on and never letting go.
It is a short word, easy to spell, difficult to define,
and impossible to live without.
Love is work, but most of all,
love is realising that every hour, every minute,
every second of it was worth it
because you did it together"

- UNKNOWN

CITAZIONE

" L'AMORE NON È PERFETTO;
NON È UNA FAVOLA O UN LIBRO DI FIABE
E NON È SEMPRE FACILE.
L'AMORE È SUPERARE GLI OSTACOLI,
AFFRONTARE LE SFIDE,
LOTTARE PER STARE INSIEME , RESISTERE E NON LASCIARE MAI ANDARE.
È UNA PAROLA BREVE,
FACILE DA PRONUNCIARE, DIFFICILE DA DEFINIRE,
E IMPOSSIBILE DI VIVERE SENZA.
L'AMORE È LAVORO, MA SOPRATTUTTO,
L'AMORE È RENDERSI CONTO CHE OGNI ORA, OGNI MINUTO,
OGNI SECONDO NE VALSE LA PENA
PERCHÉ L'AVETE FATTO INSIEME "

- ANONIMO

DISCLAIMER

It Was Always You is a work of fiction.

Although its form is that of a semi-autobiography (Gabrielle's), it is not one.

With the exception of public places any resemblance to persons living or dead is coincidental. Space and time have been rearranged to suit the convenience of the book, memory has its own story to tell.

The opinions expressed are those of the characters and should not be confused with the author's.

DICHIARAZIONE DI NON RESPONSABILITÀ

Eri Sempre Tu è un'opera di finzione.

Sebbene la sua forma sia quella del diario / semi-autobiografia, non lo è.

Ad eccezione dei luoghi pubblici, qualsiasi somiglianza con persone vive o morte è casuale. Spazio e il tempo sono stati riorganizzati per adattarsi alla comodità del libro, la memoria ha una sua storia da raccontare.

Le opinioni espresse sono quelle dei personaggi e non vanno confuse con quelle dell'autrice.

PREVIOUS IN SERIES/PRECEDENTE NELLA SERIE

The previous short story in the series is **Run to You.**

"Passport, boarding pass, reservation, all here", Gabrielle said to herself, checking her handbag to ensure she had everything.

It was finally happening. She was going to see him again. Soon.

Now she couldn't wait; she just wanted to run to him, back in his arms, once and for all.

Il racconto precedente in questa serie è **Corro da Te.**

"Passaporto, carta d'imbarco, prenotazione, tutto qui", si disse Gabrielle, controllando la borsetta per assicurarsi di avere tutto.

Stava finalmente accadendo. Lo avrebbe rivisto. Presto.

Ora non poteva aspettare; voleva solo correre da lui, di nuovo tra le sue braccia, una volta per tutte.

NEXT IN SERIES/PROSSIMO NELLA SERIE
OUT JANUARY 2025

The next short story in the series is **Her Little Secret.**

Paola has it all—a loving husband, Martin, two beautiful daughters, and a thriving career. But there's one secret she keeps hidden deep in her heart, one that threatens to unravel the life she's built. When Gabrielle, her best friend, announces her engagement to Mr. Wonderful, Paola's world begins to crumble.

As the truth slowly surfaces, Paola and Martin are forced to confront the lies that have kept them apart. Can Martin step up as the alpha Paola craves, and can Paola surrender to the love she's been afraid to fully embrace? In the midst of Gabrielle's romantic whirlwind, Paola and Martin must rediscover the passion and trust that first brought them together—or lose each other forever.

*Il prossimo racconto in questa serie è **Il Suo Piccolo Segreto.***

Paola ha tutto: un marito amorevole, Martin, due bellissime figlie e una carriera fiorente. Ma c'è un segreto che tiene nascosto nel profondo del suo cuore, uno che minaccia di distruggere la vita che si è costruita. Quando Gabrielle, la sua migliore amica, annuncia il suo fidanzamento con Mr. Wonderful, il mondo di Paola inizia a crollare.

Mentre la verità lentamente emerge, Paola e Martin sono costretti ad affrontare le bugie che li hanno tenuti separati. Riuscirà Martin a essere l'alfa che Paola desidera, e potrà Paola arrendersi all'amore che ha avuto paura di abbracciare completamente? Nel mezzo del vortice romantico di Gabrielle, Paola e Martin devono riscoprire la passione e la fiducia che li hanno uniti per primi, o perdersi per sempre.

BOOKS BY LAURA MARIANI

STOP IT! It is all in your head

Think Look Act The Part Series

Think The Part - The Workbook

Look The Part - The Workbook

Act The Part - The Workbook

Unlock Ignite & Transform Your Career

90 Days To Reboot Your Career: How To Reinvent Yourself, Your Career and Your Life

90 Days To Reboot Your Career Planner: Career Plan Journal Notebook

90 Days Coloring Book: Relaxation Stress Relief and Empowerment for Women

Unlock Ignite & Transform Your Life

I don't care if you don't like me: I LOVE ME!: 28 Ways to Love Yourself More - a Self-love book with guided practices

28 Days To Love Yourself More - Planner and Guided Journal with Prompts for Women

28 Ways to Love Yourself More Coloring Book: Relaxation and stress relief for women

Unlock Ignite & Transform Your Language Skills

Short Stories in English/Italian: Unlock Ignite & Transform Your Language Skills with Contemporary Romance - Book 1

Short Stories in English/Italian: Unlock Ignite & Transform Your Language Skills with Contemporary Romance - Book 2

Short Stories in English/Italian: Unlock Ignite & Transform Your Language Skills with Contemporary Romance - Book 3

Short Stories in English/Italian: Unlock Ignite & Transform Your Language Skills with Contemporary Romance - Book 4

Short Stories in English/Italian: Unlock Ignite & Transform Your Language Skills with Contemporary Romance - Book 5

Short Stories in English/Italian: Unlock Ignite & Transform Your Language Skills with Contemporary Romance - Book 6

Short Stories in English/Italian: Unlock Ignite & Transform Your Language Skills with Contemporary Romance - Book 7

Short Stories in English/Italian: Unlock Ignite & Transform Your Language Skills with Contemporary Romance - Book 8

Short Stories in English/Italian: Unlock Ignite & Transform Your Language Skills with Contemporary Romance - Book 9

Short Stories in English/Italian: Unlock Ignite & Transform Your Language Skills with Contemporary Romance -

Book 10

Coming September 2024

Short Stories in English/Italian: Unlock Ignite & Transform Your Language Skills with Contemporary Romance Book 11

Short Stories in English/Italian: Unlock Ignite & Transform Your Language Skills with Contemporary Romance Book 12

Short Stories in English/Italian: Unlock Ignite & Transform Your Language Skills with Contemporary Romance Book 13

Coming January 2025

Short Stories in English/Italian: Unlock Ignite & Transform Your Language Skills with Contemporary Romance Book 14

AUTHOR'S NOTE / NOTA DALL'AUTRICE

Thank you so much for reading *It Was Always You.*

Grazie mille per aver letto Eri Sempre Tu.

I hope you found reading this short story useful for *remembering* your language skills and you also enjoyed the story .

Spero che questa novella vi sia piaciuta e l'abbiate trovata utile per ricordare le vostre capacità linguistica.

A review would be much appreciated as it helps other readers discover the story and the series. Thanks.

Una recensione sarebbe molto apprezzata in quanto aiuta altri lettori a scoprire la storia e la serie. Grazie.

If you sign up for my newsletter you'll be notified of giveaways, new releases and receive personal updates from behind the scenes of my business and books.

Se ti iscrivi alla mia newsletter, sarete informati di omaggi, nuove uscite e riceverete aggiornamenti personali da dietro le quinte della mia attività e dei miei libri.

Go to/ *Visita* www.thepeoplealchemist.com to get started/ *per cominciare.*

Places in the book

I have set the story in real places in New York. You can see some of the places here:

Luoghi nel libro

Ho ambientato la storia in luoghi reali a New York. Puoi scoprire di più su di loro o anche visitare:

- Empire State Building
- The Langham, New York, Fifth Avenue

Bibliography

I read a lot of books as part of my research. Some of them together with other references include:

Bibliografia

Ho letto molti libri come parte della mia ricerca. Alcuni di loro insieme ad altri riferimenti includono:

A Theory of Human Motivation -
Abraham Maslow
Psycho-Cybernetics - **Maxwell Maltz**
Self Mastery Through Conscious Autosuggestion -

Émile Coué
The Artist Way - **Julia Cameron.**
The Complete Reader - **Neville Goddard,**
compiled and edited by **David Allen**
Tools of Titans - **Tim Ferris**

Milton Keynes UK
Ingram Content Group UK Ltd.
UKHW050825290924
1898UKWH00025B/95